*Poetry of the
Past and Present*

Poetry of the Past and Present

Ginevar Curenton

VANTAGE PRESS
New York

FIRST EDITION

All rights reserved, including the right of
reproduction in whole or in part in any form.

Copyright © 2000 by Ginevar Curenton

Published by Vantage Press, Inc.
516 West 34th Street, New York, New York 10001

Manufactured in the United States of America
ISBN: 0-533-11835-2

0 9 8 7 6 5 4 3 2 1

Contents

Preface vii
Acknowledgments ix

On Wings of Joy   1
Haiku   2
Freedom for All   3
Oh, How Gentle Love Must Be   4
A Picture of My True Love   5
The Slave Girl   6
God, Come Get Me   7
I Had a Weary Smile   8
There Appears Something in the Sky   9
Do You Remember the Autumn Colors?   10
Did You Call, My Love?   11
Paradise   12
My Little Girl   13
Wait Until Tomorrow   14
I'm Not Gonna Be Your Slave   15
The African on the Run   16
A Fool   17
The Summer Sky Glitters with Wings   18
Skyward Bound   19
Oh, How Can I Find Myself?   20
A Star Is Born   21
The Sonnet of Love   22
Black or White   23
To the Husband I Never Had   24
Love Is So Beautiful   25
A Call Beyond Thy Grave   26
To a Special Mother   27
Tear Drops   28
Love Forever   29

My Dad	30
Love Peace and Joy: A Poetical Duet	31
Randy and Maria	35

Preface

Poetry is a collection of many poems that'll lead you out of the depth of darkness and into the past, present, or future. Poems are a form of writing with rhyme and rhythm. Poems are also a way to express a million emotions.
    Poetry shifts high and low, like the wind when it blows. Poets are digging deeper and deeper than ever before, to what's in their hearts and minds. Poems are written by poets like you and me. My mind never seems to stop thinking, not even when I'm asleep. Sometimes when I awake I find myself aweeping over the beautiful lines hidden in the back of my mind. Leaving no time to write them down, words just keep popping up into my mind, bursting to come out. It's like someone shouting within my very own soul! It calls and calls and calls out to me. I can hear the echoes loud and clear, yet so pure, like a band of fairies suddenly appearing to cheer me on.
    Poetry is something that just comes naturally to a person's mind. Some poems flow like the river that never stops; it goes on and on. Sometimes words just come to me so fast, that if I pause for just a second, and a few get past me, I'm afraid it'll be too late and I'll lose the vibe.
    My poems will make you laugh, cry, yell, and scream. I hope you enjoy reading these poems as much as I enjoyed writing them.

Acknowledgments

I would like to acknowledge the following people who inspired me the most to have this book published. First I'd like to give honor and thanks to God. Next I would like to thank my mother and father, who have always been there for me, and then the best friend I've ever had, Chris. And to many, many more people whom I didn't mention, but haven't forgotten.

*Poetry of the
Past and Present*

On Wings of Joy

'Tis the air of empty flight,
Let it be my endless plight,
To soar like the angels.
And where all flying birds must go,
Chasing the rainbow through a cloudy sky,
Bound for heaven where the angels fly.
They'll be a time when my own
Wings begin to fold—
In God's arm I hope he'll hold.
I had a vision heaven was painted gold.

Haiku

Live flowers standing still,
They're a wonder of beauty
Upon a silent hill.

Freedom for All

God put us on this earth
To help each other,
Not to destroy one another.
You can lean on me.
My arms are strong.
I see no whites,
I see no blacks,
Only brothers and sisters.
God knows I'm right.

Oh, How Gentle Love Must Be

If you would
    Only reach out to me.

Just let our love be;
Release your heart
From that isolated cell.

In the heat of passion
Lies a divinity:
Peace
Of humanity.

A Picture of My True Love

Was it she who told
A picture of old,
    Lost in trash
      On a broken frame.
You only have yourself to blame.
Harvey Tate is his name.

The Slave Girl

A pretty face behind bars—
If only I could see a star.
The whites only saw
The color of my skin,
And not what lay deep within.

They held a burnin' flame
At my head,
Just before I went to bed.
"Oh! Master," I begged,
"If only one last dream.
Life is not what it seems."

God, Come Get Me

God, come get me.
Just so free I want to be.
God, come get me.

I'm blind, please let me see.
God, come get me.
Art Thou a tree for me to see?

God, come get me.

I Had a Weary Smile

I walked a weary mile.
    I had fear in my heart
And tears in my eyes.

I paused and heard an echo
    In the wind. It said,
"Until death do us part."

Heaven is the only joy;
    I had only two wishes,
The gold fish, my old toy,

    And my grand baby boy.

There Appears Something in the Sky

Like an angel flying toward heaven above,
It ascends in the sky, like a dove.
Then it vanished out of sight.

I steer up towards the sky,
Why? I do not know
What God wished to show.

The sun was shining bright,
Not even a cloud in sight.
The sky is blue, what I've seen is true.

Do You Remember the Autumn Colors?

    Autumn colors
Are golden brown,
    Brown.
Yellow and green,
Red and orange,
    Who said they would turn?
"Not I," said the huge orange
    Pumpkin.
"Not I," said the yellow corn,
    "It must've been the acorn."

Did You Call, My Love?

The voice I heard sounds just like yours.
   I heard the wind echo!
The voice echoed far, far away.
   Your love I've never refused.
Had I to choose, only your love, I could use.
   These invincible hands I couldn't understand, crawling up and down my body; this secret is for keeps. Oh! How I wept. The pleasure soon vanished. I grieved as he spoke in Spanish, "I love you." The joy and pain I could never ever explain. "You left me a baby boy; the joy in my heart lingers on and on—
   "Nothing shall ever keep us apart," the voice said. "Trust me. I'm yours forever and ever, my love, my love."

Paradise

Poets die like anyone else,
Yet they should wonder.
I saw his spirit rise over yonder,
By a stone of pure gold
Upon a lovely hillside.
It begins to "glow and glow."
I could not help but notice it.
Oh! God, behold this poet.
Sitting there with a warm and gentle smile.
I could hear the song of a million fireflies,
And the cry of crickets.
He disappeared in the night before my eyes.

My Little Girl

I never saw anyone like her.
When I call she's always near.
She's just a lovely dear.
No one else is like my little
Girl, not in this world.

Wait Until Tomorrow

My love,
I put you above
All of my friends;
You're in my every dream.
I want to spend the
Rest of my life with
Only you.
Oh! God, I pray
That my dream comes
True.
If not I'll feel
So blue, but I'll never
Stop loving you.

I'm Not Gonna Be Your Slave

I'll be carried to my grave.
I'll be strong and brave.
I'll be strong and brave.

God is my shield;
He's for real.

You made my days and nights foggy,
But God made them clear.
God is here. I can feel him near.

You lash me for the work I've done.
You'll shoot me if I run,
Though I work from sun till sun
From Africa black as night,
I'm the speck of light.

The African on the Run

Strong as a lion, he ran through
The bushes. And he ran through the
Briers.

Darker he than any leopard's spot.
On his trail they kept hot,
But which one they know not.

A Fool

Trying not to understand,
    He will stand
    Upon his hands
    Instead of his feet.

    Dishonor
    And
    Honor
    Not,

    Disgrace
    But
    Not
An honest face,
    Lips that sting, with strife,

    And words that sting
    With the wrong advice,
    That destroy in shame,
    That's a fool's game.

The Summer Sky Glitters with Wings

In my heart I heard 'em sing,
As they flew, one by one, flappin'
Their wings.

In a distant sky
"Higher and higher" the birds fly,

Till, out of sight,
In the mist of night,
With a thousand birds in flight,

Easing in and out of sight,
They came to rest at the mid of night,
Flappin' their wings from side to side.

Skyward Bound

I often wonder what's beneath the sky—
    I cannot tell you why?
In a distance far and near,
Fly once high above the ocean shore,

Till you met the land of make believe,
    And a city you thought you'd
    Never see,
    And all the wonder you thought
    There'd be.

Oh, How Can I Find Myself?

I don't know how to explain.
Oh, I'm so ashamed.
Oh, will someone please help me to understand?
Jesus! Jesus! Is the one who
Can. With his powerful hands, He
Created the whole land.

A Star Is Born

Jesus sent his holy angels
    After me.
I'm not the one—
Must I be?
I cried out, "O Father,
O Father.
    Why oh, why me?
Am I the only one? Would
You truly agree? Why
Not three,
    For the one of me?"

The Sonnet of Love

Must thou love me for love?
A stone of fire, a flame of sweat,
You're my heart's desire—
      The power of love is great;
Though slaking thirst for a brook,
Just one look
      was all it took.
We love the way we ought.
A lesson of love he taught.
Your love I hope to gain
      without any shame.
The power of love is so
Gentle to the mind.
Love is a mystery.

Black or White

Wherever you may go,
        My love
Will always show.

No matter whether
You're "black or white,"
Your love shall forever be.

It matters not the color of your skin,
Nor the texture within—
This is my opinion, one I recommend.

No one can ever change what I see
In thee; it's a free choice between
You and me. Black is "beautiful," and

So is "white." Mix them together.
It will make a wonderful combination.
Some will question. Some will ask, "Why
Not?" Some will say that should never be.
But we'll see.

To the Husband I Never Had

I think of fun
We could have had—
And a race we
Could've run.
>Or just breathing in the sun.
>Oh! I miss the page from the love letter
>You never wrote.

I'm young in age—
Not once engaged,
In search for a husband
Who's long overdue.
>The love I hold in my heart,
>Just for you,
>For the husband I never knew,

Untouched by the husband I never had.
Oh! I dream of loving you so much.

Love Is So Beautiful
(To the one I love, Chris)

Love is! Love is! So rare.
And so hard to bear.
Love is! Love is!
Oh how beautiful love must be
To the one who really must care,
And the one who's willing to share.
My love grows stronger for thee.
Together we've watched the glittering moon.
Why? O! Why, did it fade so soon?
Love must linger, O honey; I dream of thee.
In your arms I'd love to be
In my heart I remember
Love is! Love is! Holding your hand.
Love is! Love is! Smelling your perfume,
While making plans.
Love is joy. Love is meant to be.

A Call Beyond Thy Grave

I could hear my loved one callin',
And callin' from the grave!
    Bold and brave.
    Bold and brave.

Time rush away!
I saw them fade into a flower.
On that very special day.

I can see 'em in the early
Mornin' dewlike shower.
Even after hours.
Even after hours.

To a Special Mother

It's good to share the gift of love.
God is watchin' from above,
He bring about many, many, thing.

Mother when there was a
Problem, you would always say
I understand.

You were very gentle with your
Commands.
You have a very kind
Generosity with love and
Warmth.

The love and joy I appreciate,
Go now and celebrate
Many years of motherhood.

Tear Drops

Tear drop, tear drop, from my
Grandson's eyes, he looked so shy.
His mother made him cry!
He ran to his granny.
To his mother he waved good-bye.

Love Forever

Love is neat
And
Twice as nice.
Just like white on rice.
It's like water without the ice,
Love gives you pleasure
That can never be measured.

My Dad

Who stood so strong and tall!
I truly remember it all.
Through my young childhood, one
    So small.
Remember it all,
I learned after I got grown
And left my father home
That he was'n my dad at all.
I love him so, so, much.
    I ask myself, time and
Time again how could this be?
Or why did it happen to me?
A secret unfold, is a secret untold.
If he ever found out that I'm
Not his natural child he'd be mad
And I'd be sad.
Sometimes love is hidden, like the moon.
Yet you know it's always there.
In the dark somewhere, out there.

Love Peace and Joy: A Poetical Duet

I.

Him

You took me away from my isolated
Cell my technicolor conformity.
Let my arms provide you shelter
My love! My love! You mean so much to me.

Her

It was love at first sight, sight oh!
What a beautiful night. My love! My love!
You never once refused.
You were sent from heaven above.

Him

Once upon a time, I cheated myself.
With illusions of power and self-
Centered glory. Until you held me tight,
Tight and took away my days of fabricated
Stories.

Her

Your love, your love, was pure from the very
Start a night-in-gale, a night-in-gale
Touching my heart. I could see stars glowin'
In your eyes. I could see love in your smile.

II.

Him

No one but "God," could count the miles, miles.
I would run to you my one and only love.
From heaven above, my true love I finally meet.
Someone who needs me, like I need you.

Her

God must have sent you from heaven above.
You've charmed me with words.
Now charm me with your love, love you've
Touched the deepest place in my heart.

Him

I feel oh so good within your arms I
Feel like a dove bathin' in the sunlight.
Who flew to your door to change your tears to
Ink and your blues to pink as well as brighten
Your night.

Her

My handsome Prince my baby blue who
Kneeled at my feet, an answer to a dream
Come true. I moan softly oh kiss me! Oh
Kiss! One more time if your love is true.

Him

Upon this day we pledge our love for each
Other. My love there will be no other.
When you're feelin' blue, call and I'll come
A runnin'. Let us seal our love with a kiss.

III.

Her

I'm falling in love, I'm falling
In love, with a handsome Prince.
A night-in-gale! A night-in-gale!
Touching my heart. No one will ever
Keep us apart.

Him and Her "Together"

Our nightmares will vanish,
Our love will never die. May heaven
Unite us. And may the sunshine ever be
So bright. Upon you and I for the two
Of us finally forever one, my love,
My love we are as one.

Randy and Maria

I.

Two turtle doves,
Setting in a nearby tree
Just as lovely as can be.

Two hearts young and free!
Two hearts young and free!

Which direction will they fly?

Yet thy wings said good-bye,
Yet thy wings said good-bye.

To that place their hearts desire.
Like melting fire! Like melting
Fire!

I can see the love and affection
Between those two. Up! Up! They
Both flew. Up! Up! They both flew.

II.

Two turtle doves, are very much
In love. They flew back to that
Same ol' tree as merry as can
Be. Kissing her lover saying good-bye.
Kissing her lover saying good-bye.
Up! Up! And away they fly.